SEE INSIDE

A SUBMARINE

Series Editor: **R. J. Unstead**

KINGFISHER BOOKS

Series Editor
R. J. Unstead

Author
Jonathan Rutland

Adviser
Lt. Cdr Francis Worthington, RN

Illustrators
Roger Full, Ron Jobson,
Paul Wright, Mike Saunders,
Temple Art

Kingfisher Books, Grisewood & Dempsey Ltd,
Elsley House, 24–30 Great Titchfield Street,
London W1P 7AD

This revised edition published in 1988
by Kingfisher Books
Originally published in hardcover in 1980
by Hutchinson & Co (Publishers) Ltd

BRITISH LIBRARY CATALOGUING IN PUBLICATION DATA
Rutland, Jonathan
See inside a submarine.—2nd ed.—
(See inside)
1. Submarine boats—Juvenile literature
I. Title II. Full, Roger III. Sington, Adrian
623.8'257 V857
ISBN 0 86272 346 9

Printed in Hong Kong

CONTENTS

A British Porpoise class submarine. This is a diesel-electric powered design, very similar to the Oberon class. Such older types of craft are still useful in the nuclear age, because they can operate underwater in almost total silence. Nuclear submarines must keep their cooling systems running, which produces a tell-tale noise.

Early Submarines

Nuclear-powered submarines like the one described in this book are probably the deadliest of all war machines. Many roam the world's oceans unseen and unheard, carrying missiles with a range of over 4000 km (2500 miles).

From the earliest times inventors have dreamed of warships that could attack from beneath the sea. The first craft to travel underwater successfully was built in England in the 1620s. It had a wooden frame covered with leather and was propelled by oars which fitted snugly through holes in the leather skin.

The first purpose-built warship submarine–the *Turtle*–was launched in America during the War of Independence in 1775. The *Turtle*'s one-man crew manoeuvred this secret new weapon under the British ship. When it came to hand-drilling holes in its hull to place explosive charges, the mission failed. The British man-of-war had a copper hull. The first submarine to sink an enemy ship was during the American Civil War. In 1864 the Confederate submarine *Hunley* ram-torpedoed and sank the Federal *Housatonic*. But the explosion destroyed the *Hunley* too.

The French *Narval* was one of the first really practical submarines. Launched in 1899, it was small with a crew of seven. Like all early powered submarines, it had two sets of propulsion machinery. Diesel engines propelled the craft on the surface. The same engines also charged the batteries which powered the electric motors used for underwater propulsion. As the batteries needed recharging often, these early submarines spent most of their time on the surface. But they worked, and armed with self-propelled torpedoes, they were useful war machines–the true ancestors of our modern submarines.

The one-man operated Turtle*–the first submarine to be used, unsuccessfully, in combat during the American War of Independence.*

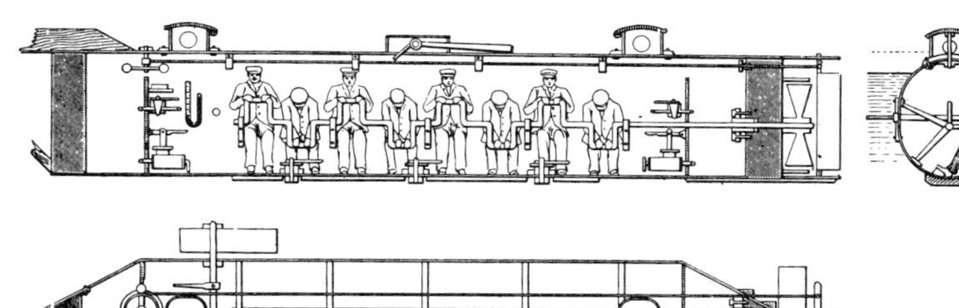

The American Hunley *was powered by eight men cranking a propeller. The boat was very unstable and such a large crew made the interior hot and unpleasant. Used by the Confederates in the American Civil War, it managed to sink an enemy sloop. But the explosion also sank the* Hunley, *killing all her crew.*

Above: The Resurgam *was invented by a Liverpool clergyman, William Garret in 1879. It was powered by steam, but in trials off the Welsh coast, it sank with a crew of three on board.*

Below: The French submarine cruiser, Surcouf *(1932) was designed to travel fast on the surface as well as submerged. It carried a sea-plane, a boarding boat for surface action and 80 torpedoes!*

The Nuclear Submarine

The first nuclear-powered submarine, *Nautilus*, was launched in the USA in 1954. On her first voyage she broke all records by travelling 5000 km (3000 miles) without surfacing or refuelling. Nuclear submarines can stay so long submerged because their nuclear reactors do not produce poisonous exhaust fumes. Conventional, petrol-powered submarines must surface frequently to release exhaust gases. As for refuelling, an average nuclear submarine can go about seven times around the world on a tiny amount of uranium fuel – about the size of a golf ball.

The ballast tanks, *the spaces between the inner hull and outer hull, stretch from stern of the missile room to the propeller and forward of the fin to the bows. By filling or emptying these tanks, the submarine rises or falls.*

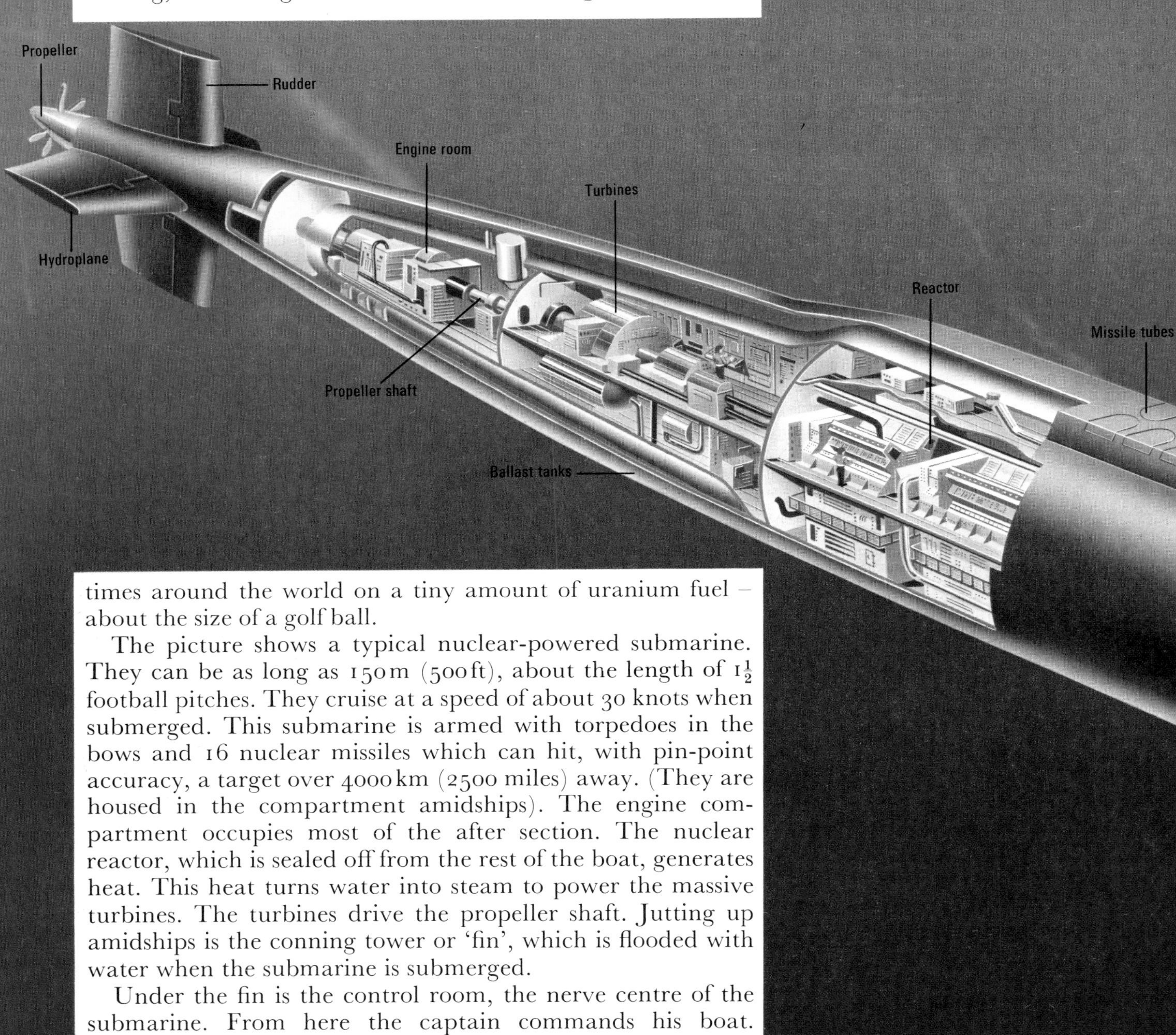

The picture shows a typical nuclear-powered submarine. They can be as long as 150 m (500 ft), about the length of 1½ football pitches. They cruise at a speed of about 30 knots when submerged. This submarine is armed with torpedoes in the bows and 16 nuclear missiles which can hit, with pin-point accuracy, a target over 4000 km (2500 miles) away. (They are housed in the compartment amidships). The engine compartment occupies most of the after section. The nuclear reactor, which is sealed off from the rest of the boat, generates heat. This heat turns water into steam to power the massive turbines. The turbines drive the propeller shaft. Jutting up amidships is the conning tower or 'fin', which is flooded with water when the submarine is submerged.

Under the fin is the control room, the nerve centre of the submarine. From here the captain commands his boat. Between the control room and the torpedo compartment are the living quarters for the 150-strong crew. A submarine is no pleasure cruiser as the quarters are cramped. Most of the space is taken up by the tons of stores, equipment and machinery.

To dive, the captain gives the order 'open main vents'. The ballast tanks, the spaces between the inner and outer hull, are then flooded with sea water so that the submarine sinks (1). To surface (2), water is expelled from the ballast tanks by compressed air. As the the submarine becomes more buoyant, it rises.

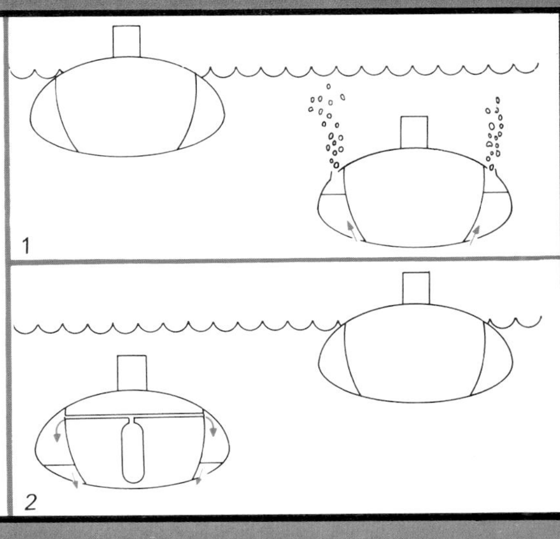

When the submarine, or boat as submariners call their craft, is on the surface, the captain commands from the bridge on top of the fin. The fin also houses the attack and search periscopes, a radar and radio mast, and two snorkels for use in emergencies.

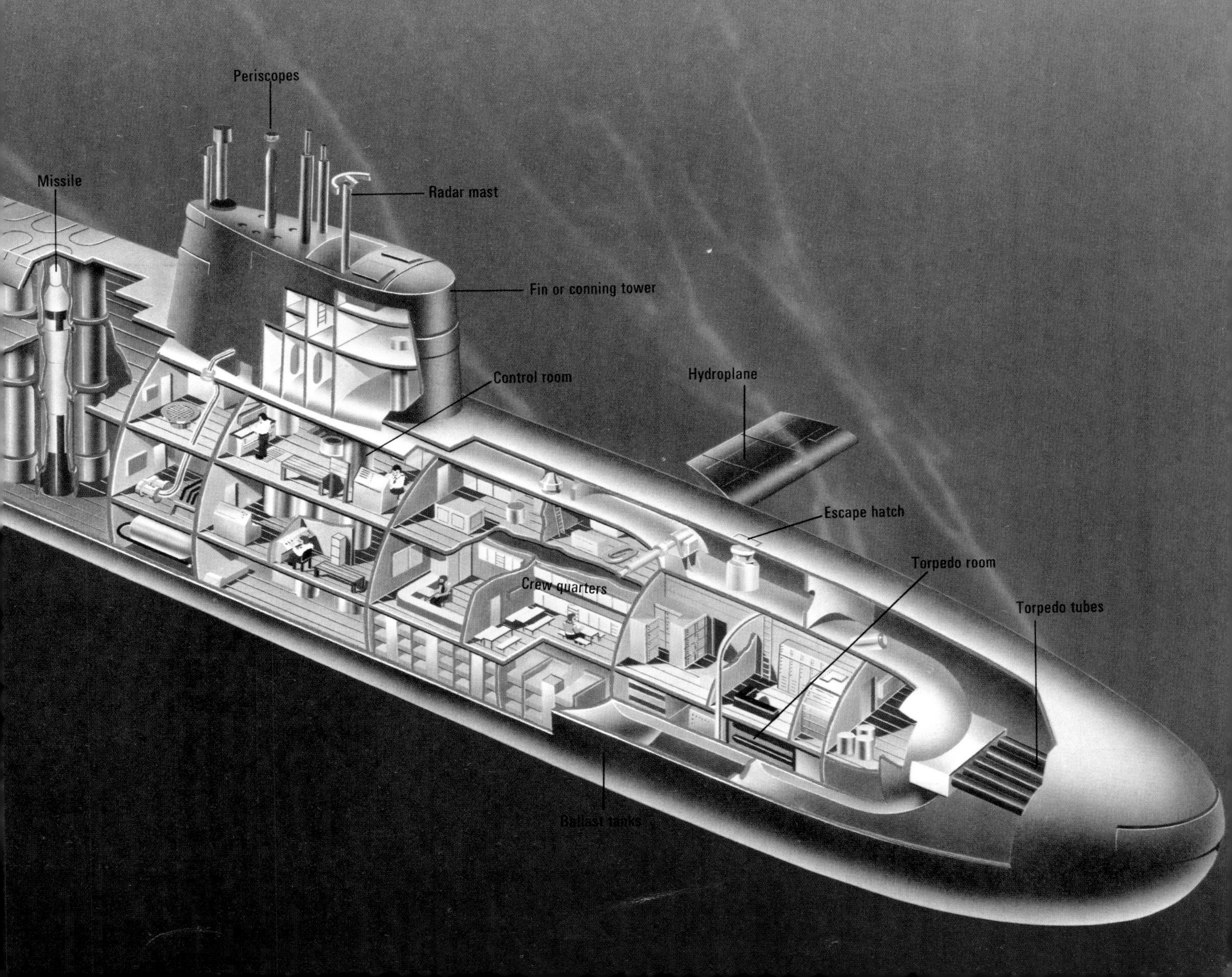

Periscope
Planesmen
Radar operator
Captain
Senior officer

The Control Room

The boat is near the surface so that the captain can use his periscope. The radar operator is checking his scanner to confirm that there are no enemy ships or aircraft nearby. A senior officer oversees the two planesmen, to see that everything is operating smoothly.

The picture shows a cutaway of the conning tower or 'fin' and the control room. This is the captain's command post. Here he is scouring the horizon through his search periscope. So that he can be in constant touch, he has a cabin in the control room itself.

Before diving, the submarine must be checked for 'tightness'. All hatches are shut and 'clipped'. By now, the officer at the Control Panel has checked and adjusted the internal tanks. These can be pumped more or less full of water to keep the boat in a state of neutral buoyancy. This means that the boat sits suspended in the water without rising or descending. For example, when a torpedo is fired, water must be added to restore the balance, because without this, the boat would be sluggish to control.

When all is well, the captain gives the command: 'Open main vents'. Water fills the main ballast tanks, and the submarine sinks just below the surface. From now on the submarine 'flies' through the water much as an aircraft flies through the air. Its flight is controlled by small 'wings' called hydroplanes and by the vertical tail fin or rudder.

Two planesmen, or 'drivers', control the boat. They operate control columns very similar to those on an aeroplane. The one on the left is a petty officer and controls the more important aft (stern) hydroplanes. He is assisted by a leading seaman who handles the rudder and forward hydroplanes. With hydroplanes angled for diving, and the propeller turning, the submarine moves forward and downward.

The driver cannot see where he is going, so he relies on instruments to show him his position. It is easy to lose all sense of direction. The most up-to-date submarines have a computerized navigation system: an electronic screen shows a 'roadway' straight ahead, and the craft's attitude to the imaginary road.

A simplified diagram to show how the periscope works. Inside the angled top cover is a prism (A) to turn the image round the corner. This can be tilted to view the sea or sky. The whole periscope can be rotated for all-round vision. At the foot of the tube another prism (B) bends the image towards the eyepiece. Lenses in between make the image sharp and large. There is a large periscope and a small one, difficult to detect from the air.

There are two sets of hydroplanes, one forward and the other aft. To dive, the aft hydroplanes are angled up and the forward ones down (1). This forces the submarine's stern up and the bow down. To rise, the hydroplanes are angled the opposite way (2).

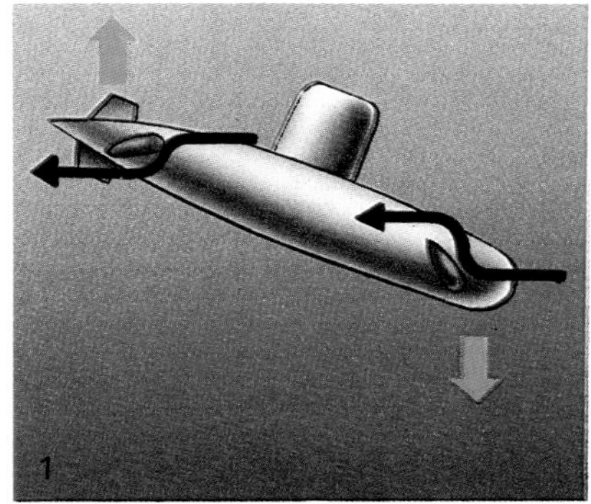

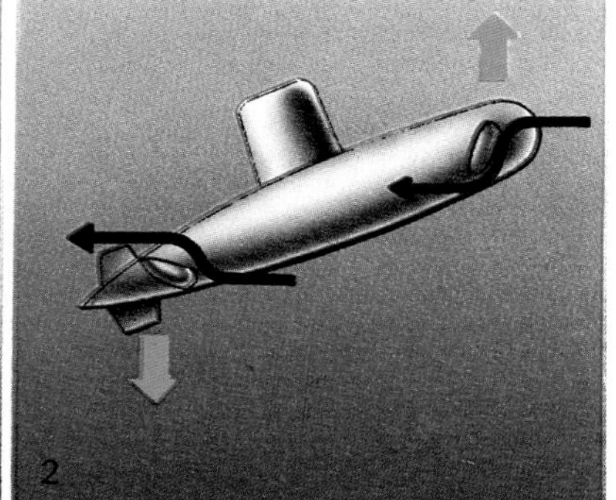

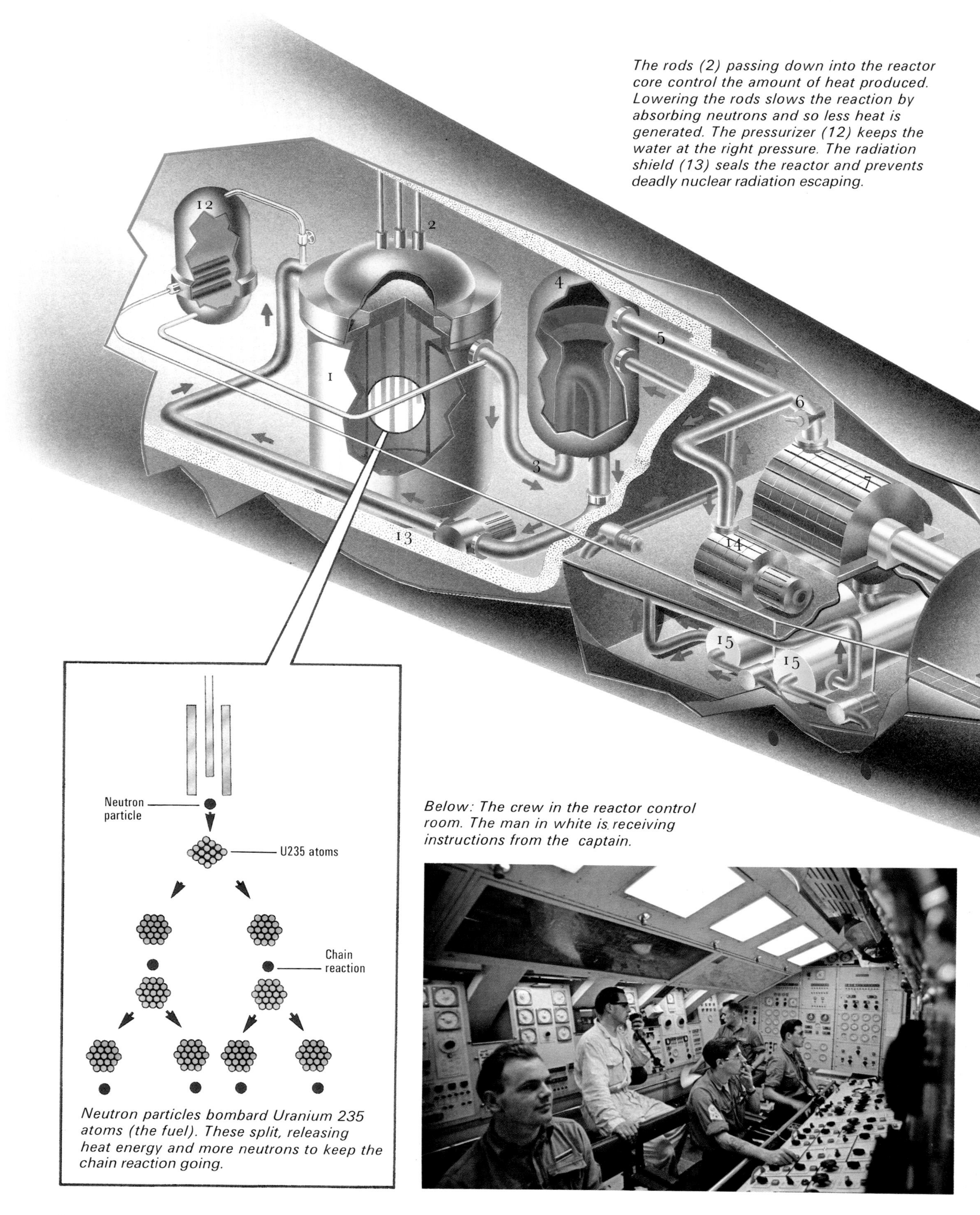

The rods (2) passing down into the reactor core control the amount of heat produced. Lowering the rods slows the reaction by absorbing neutrons and so less heat is generated. The pressurizer (12) keeps the water at the right pressure. The radiation shield (13) seals the reactor and prevents deadly nuclear radiation escaping.

Neutron particles bombard Uranium 235 atoms (the fuel). These split, releasing heat energy and more neutrons to keep the chain reaction going.

Below: The crew in the reactor control room. The man in white is receiving instructions from the captain.

Engines and Power

The submarine's source of energy is its nuclear reactor (1). The diagram (bottom left) shows how the fuel–Uranium 235–is bombarded with neutrons to produce heat energy. The nuclear reactor takes the place of a conventional boiler. Control rods (2) are fitted to adjust the amount of heat produced (see caption). Heat from the reactor is used to heat water which flows in a sealed circuit (3) around it. This primary circuit heats water in the steam generator (4). Here the primary hot water heats the secondary circuit (5) which produces steam.

The steam rises to the top of the steam generator and passes to the throttle (6). The wider it is opened, the more steam passes through, and the faster the engine turns. From the throttle the steam goes to the main steam turbine engine (7). This is basically the same as the engines used in great liners of 50 years ago, and in modern oil tankers. The jet of steam turns the blades or vanes in the turbine much as wind turns a windmill. Turbines are most efficient when spinning at high speeds. Propellers are only efficient at low speeds. So a reduction gear (8) is needed to reduce the speed of rotation. To the right of the reduction gear is the clutch (9), and to the right of that an electric propulsion motor (10). This runs off batteries. It can be used in an emergency. Or it may be needed when operating close to the enemy, as it makes very little noise. The submarine is fitted with conventional diesel engines to generate electricity when in port, and to provide power should the nuclear reactor fail.

The thrust block (11) just to the left of the propeller holds the propeller shaft firmly in position.

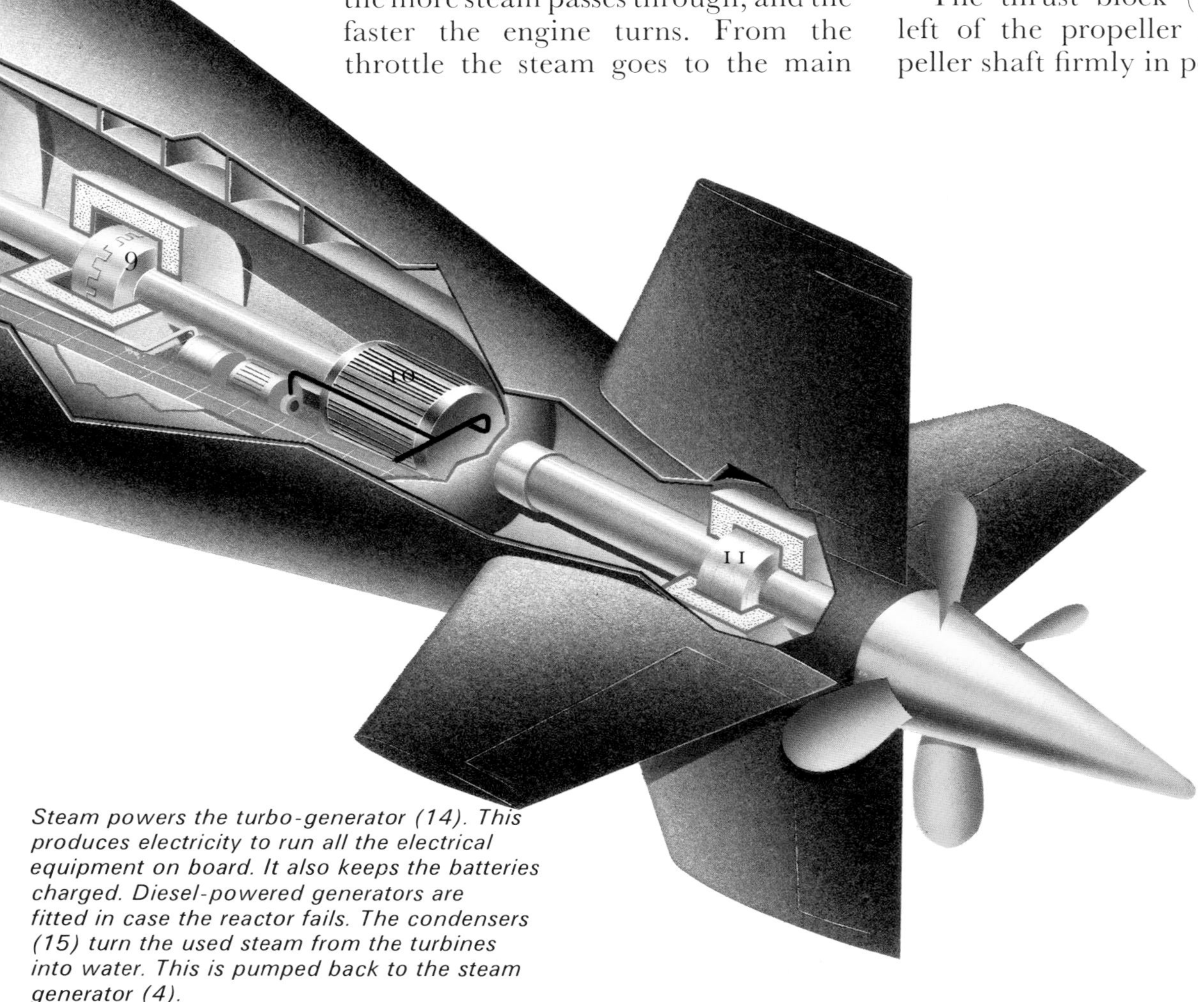

Steam powers the turbo-generator (14). This produces electricity to run all the electrical equipment on board. It also keeps the batteries charged. Diesel-powered generators are fitted in case the reactor fails. The condensers (15) turn the used steam from the turbines into water. This is pumped back to the steam generator (4).

STEERING BY THE STARS

Celestial navigation relies on measuring the position of the stars, or sun. The equipment needed is shown in the picture. A sextant is also needed. This measures the angle of a star from the vertical or from the horizon. The navigator also needs tables to show at what point a star is directly overhead at any given moment. He measures the star's angle from his position. He can then calculate how far he is from the place where it is directly overhead. Navigation satellites orbit the earth transmitting radio beams. With special equipment the navigator can use these to fix his position.

Setting their Course

Conventional submarines have to ascend to snorkel depth (see page 15) regularly for air. From just below the surface they can use periscope and radio to fix their position, or celestial and satellite navigation (see box above). But it also puts them at risk, as they may be detected by enemy ships or aircraft. Nuclear submarines patrol deep underwater for weeks on end without ever needing to approach the surface. They are almost impossible to detect. But their secrecy gives them new problems in navigation and communication. Scientists had to find a method by which nuclear submarines could keep track of their position without giving themselves away to the enemy. The answer was to devise a modern computerized version of one of the oldest and most widely used navigation systems of all – dead reckoning.

The basic idea is simple. If you know your starting point, and you know how far you have travelled and in what direction, you can work out your new position. To ancient seafarers dead reckoning was an art, helped by some very simple equipment. To nuclear submariners, it has become a science using the latest technology. The method is called *inertial navigation*. It is amazingly accurate, and enables a submarine to voyage fully around the world and return to its starting point. In fact it is usual to ascend to periscope depth occasionally during a voyage, just to check. Inertial navigation uses gyroscopes and accelerometers to measure every change in the ship's speed and direction.

Charts of the seabed have been made for many years. When cruising in these regions the submarine can navigate by using the charts and an echo sounder.

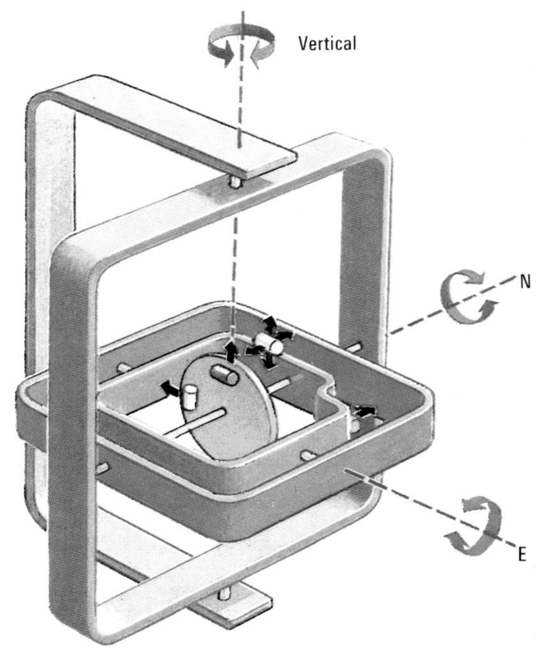

The ship's inertial navigational system – SINS – tells the commander exactly where he is at any time. Gyroscopes keep one section of the frame pointing north, one east and the third one straight up. When the boat alters course or speed, the frames try to change with it. They cannot. The gyroscopes stop them. Accelerometers measure the strength of the force trying to turn each of the three frames. A computer uses these measurements to calculate exactly how far the boat has moved, and in what direction.

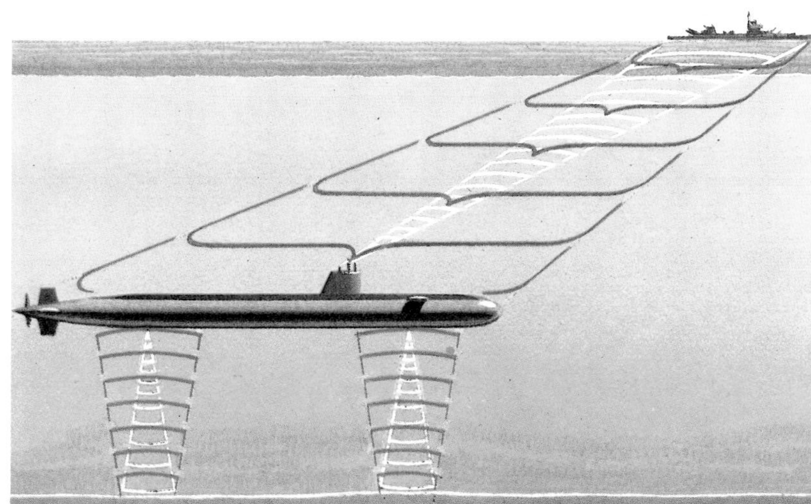

SOUND DETECTION

Sonar is an electronic system for picking up sounds underwater. There are two types: passive sonar, which simply picks up all sounds in the area (upper diagram); and active sonar, which transmits pings of sound and receives the returning echoes (lower diagram). The ping may bounce back off another ship. The time it takes to return, and its direction, pinpoint the enemy's position. Or it may be used in echo sounding–bouncing the sound off the sea bed to find the depth, and exact shape of the sea bed.

Active sonar has one great disadvantage. Its pings may be picked up by enemy sonar. So submarines today rely mainly on passive sonar. With the help of additional equipment, passive sonar can pick up sounds from other ships, and calculate their precise range and direction. The submarine can therefore locate an enemy craft, and follow or destroy it without giving its own position away.

RADAR AND RADIO

Radar is similar to active sonar, but transmits radio pulses instead of sound. It is widely used by aircraft and surface ships for seeing the way at night–the pattern of echoes form an electronic picture of the view ahead. However, radio signals cannot be transmitted underwater. Submarines can only use radar when the radar aerial can be projected above the water. Then it is valuable for detecting aircraft. But it is also liable to give the submarine's own position away on an enemy's radar.

Radio waves at very low frequency (VLF) can be picked up by a submarine using a trailing aerial. To keep in touch with its base, the submarine may release a communications buoy which floats to the surface. Signals from the buoy are picked up by an aircraft. To radio direct to base, the submarine must come up so that its main aerial is above water.

Action Stations!

The captain's finger at the ready on the missile firing button. The missile cannot be fired by accident. It requires a complex sequence of commands from headquarters and actions by the captain and other officers.

There are two main types of nuclear-powered naval submarines. Each has a totally different job to do. The first, the one described in this book, is the missile submarine. It also carries torpedoes, but its principal task has nothing to do with war at sea. It is used as a mobile missile launching platform. The huge missiles have ranges of many thousands of kilometres. Each one is powerful enough to destroy a city.

The missiles are launched from underwater. If one country considered starting a war, it would know that the enemy's missile submarines were waiting to fire their missiles. Knowing it could not destroy the enemy's submarines first because it could not find them, there would be no point in one country starting a war as it too would be destroyed. This idea is known as *nuclear deterrence*.

The other type of naval submarine is the fleet or attack submarine. This is one of the navy's main attack vessels. It is armed with anti-submarine and anti-ship missiles (these rise up out of the water and dive down on their targets). Attack submarines are smaller than the missile types, with a crew of 100. They are also faster. In the event of war, their task would be to patrol the oceans unseen, seeking and shadowing or destroying enemy submarines and ships.

Attack submarines could be used in a small-scale war. But their main purpose is as hunter-killers in a full-scale war. So, like their bigger brothers, everyone hopes they never see action.

Right: The torpedo compartment during action. A torpedo has just been fired. It is aimed at the ship dropping the depth charges. One can be seen exploding close to the boat's hull.

TORPEDO

Propeller

Electric motor

Warhead

MISSILE

Rocket motor

Multiple warheads

MISSILES AND TORPEDOES

The submarine's main armament are torpedoes (above) and missiles. The torpedo is driven by a built-in electric motor and travels at around 60kph (40mph). Some carry sonar equipment to guide them to the target. Others trail a thin wire, along which commands can be 'telephoned' from the mother submarine.

The missile shown is a Polaris type, designed for destroying distant targets on land. It is 10m (33ft) long, weighs 30,000kg (65,000lb) has a range of 4500km (2800 miles), and is fitted with nuclear explosives. The missile is launched by gas or air pressure. On reaching the surface, its rocket motor ignites, and a built-in inertial navigation system guides it precisely to its target.

ANTI-SUBMARINE WARFARE

While fully submerged, the nuclear submarine has little fear of attack. But, when at periscope depth it may be detected by enemy aircraft, helicopters and ships. These carry radar and sonar equipment to locate submarines and a host of weapons with which to bombard them. Special ASW (anti-submarine warfare) aircraft have a sonar receiver on the end of a cable. This can be trailed in the water and may detect a submarine. Ships carry depth-charges. These underwater bombs are lobbed into the water and sink downwards. They are pre-set to explode close to the submarine.

The SLBM (Submarine-Launched Ballistic Missile) is the main offensive weapon carried by submarines. Here is a Trident missile being test-fired by a submerged US Navy submarine. Each Trident carries eight independently targeted warheads.

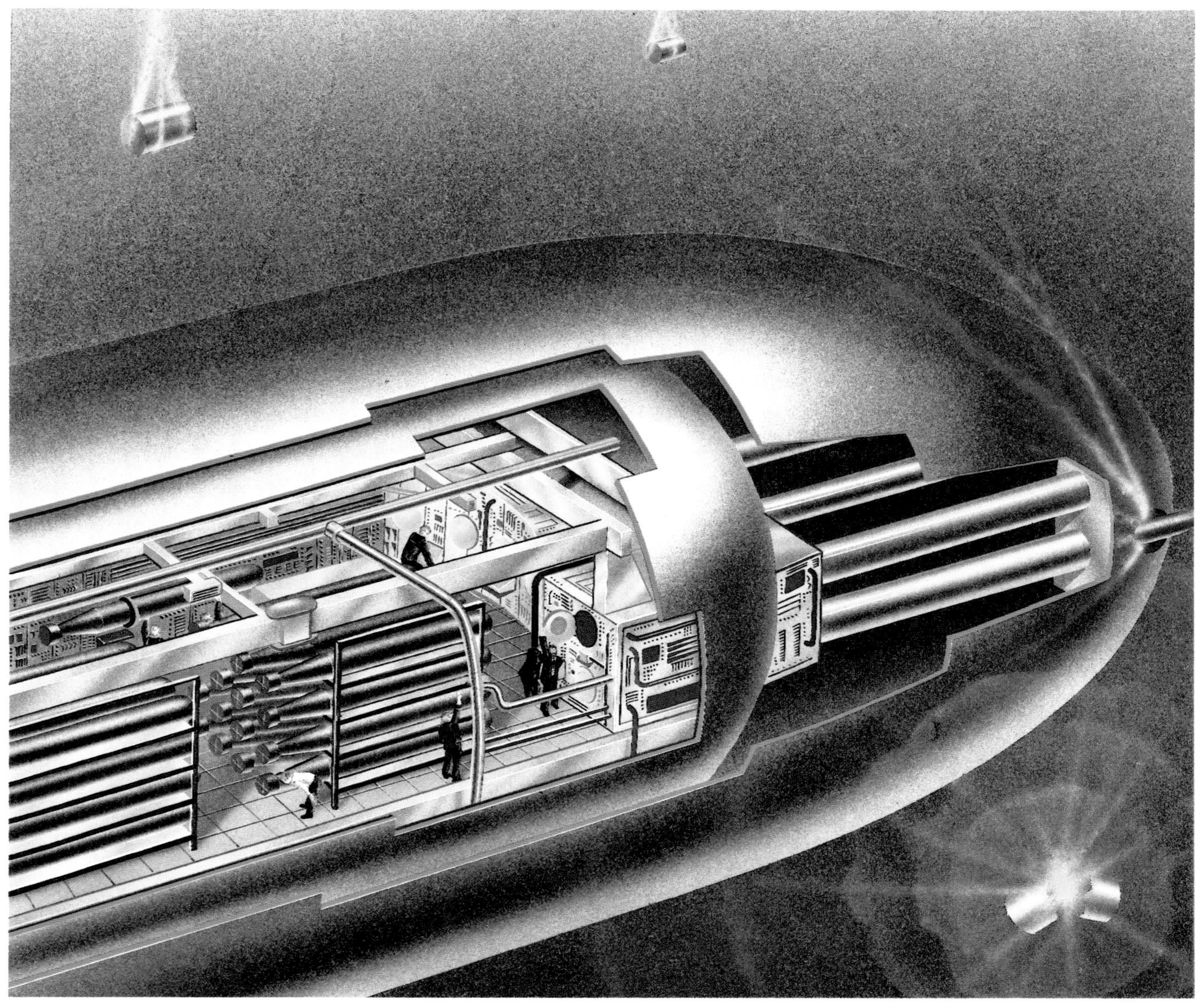

The Royal Navy fleet submarine HMS Swiftsure *on the surface near its base in Faslane, Scotland.*

On Duty

Each missile submarine has two crews, one on duty, the other on leave. The two are known in Britain as Port and Starboard, and in the USA as Blue and Gold. There are around a dozen officers, 55 senior ratings and 75 junior ratings.

Each patrol lasts six weeks or more. After diving, the craft heads for the stretch of ocean where it is stationed. Only the captain and a few of his officers know where this is. There are always routine jobs involved in running any craft – cooking, cleaning, navigation, keeping a constant alert for faults of all kinds, including leaks, and tending the engines. Both nuclear reactor and turbines are operated from control rooms containing a mass of dials and switches. Engine maintenance is completed between patrols, but occasionally faults develop which must be corrected.

Then there are tasks special to nuclear missile submarines. These include ensuring that everything is safe and in order in the missile centre. In the reactor, routine checks are made by medical staff with a geiger counter to test for radiation leaks. As an added precaution, the crew wear 'radiation badges' containing a film sensitive to radiation. Then there is rubbish to eject. It is sealed in metal containers and sent overboard through the garbage ejector.

Occasionally, during the patrol there will be a missile firing practice. When the order from shore HQ arrives, the entire boat is put on 'action stations missile'. All procedures are tested short of an actual missile launch.

LIFE SUPPORT

All submarines are equipped with a pair of breathing tubes called snorkels or snorts. These are normally retracted inside the fin. In operation, the tube rises above the water, the float drops (upper diagram) opening the cover. When below the surface, the hollow float presses up, forcing a tightly fitting cover over the top of the tube (lower diagram). Nuclear submarines need their snorkels only in an emergency. Both fresh air and water are made on board. Power to drive the special equipment comes from the turbo-generator. Two distillers make 5000 gallons of fresh water a day, by boiling sea water and collecting the steam, which is fresh. Fresh air is made by *electrolysis* (passing electricity through fresh water).One pint of water produces air for the crew for one hour. The atmosphere control officer sees that just the right amount of oxygen is put into the air (too much is nearly as dangerous as too little). Devices called 'scrubbers' absorb the stale gases from the air.

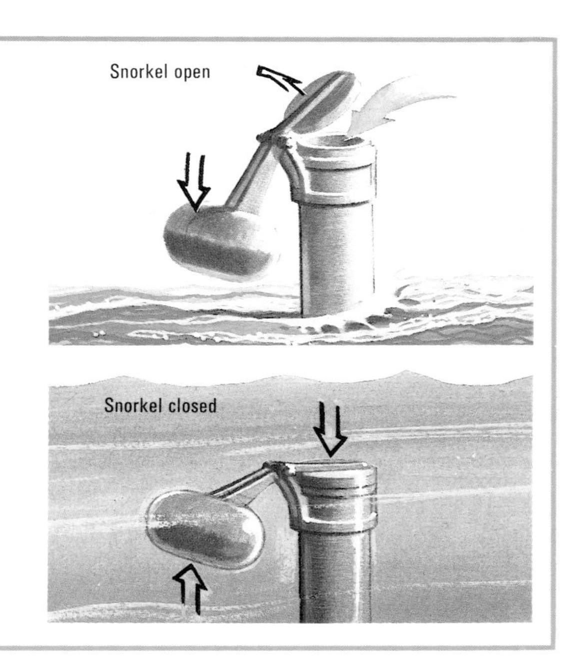

Below: Faults and minor accidents occur on even the best built and run craft. Three of the crew in frogmen's suits are untangling a metal hawser from one of the screws with oxy-acetylene torches.

Off Watch

Nuclear missile submarines are much larger than other types, but most of their huge hull is packed full of equipment, machinery and weapons. The crew's living accommodation is comfortable, but not very spacious. The captain and his officers all have cabins. Ratings have cubicles – each containing a bunk and a locker.

There are separate dining halls, lounges and libraries for officers and ratings. This represents a great luxury and advance. Earlier conventional submarines had no space for rooms reserved just for relaxation. Even so, there is no room for sports of any kind; their main forms of relaxation include board and card games – chess, bridge and ludo are favourites in the Royal Navy. Then there is the cinema. A different film is shown each evening, and the crew often see new films before their friends and relatives ashore. Regular television and radio broadcasts cannot be received, but closed circuit television sets show a good variety of programmes. Many crew members spend much of their spare time studying by correspondence course for examinations, and many have hobbies they can follow at sea.

The food is always excellent, with a wide selection to choose from. Someone calculated that the provisions taken on board before a patrol, would feed a family of four for six years! Meals for officers and ratings are the same. Steak and chips is the favourite.

Radio messages can be received, and relatives on shore are allowed to send a 40-word 'gram' a week. Another weekly event is the publication of the submarine's newspaper. This is usually lighthearted and for everyone's amusement.

Two factors make life aboard a submarine very different from that on a surface ship. One is the absence of a natural night and day. The only way of telling night from day is by the red lights used at night. This is to accustom the crew's eyes to dim light – in case the periscope must be used.

The other great difference is the lack of space, which has one strange effect. For the six weeks or so of a patrol the men never see anything more than four or five metres (15 ft) distant. When they leave the ship at the end of a patrol their eyes cannot easily focus on distant objects. One submariner had to ask for help crossing a road on his first day ashore. And care must be taken when driving in the first few days ashore.

Officers relaxing in the ward room. On Sundays a church service is held here.

Right: The French Redoubtable, a nuclear submarine. Like all submariners, its crews spend many weeks at sea, mostly underwater. To combat boredom, many activities are organized – a different film is shown every evening, and crews can keep fit in the health room. The small pictures show life on board a Royal Navy nuclear submarine. Top left: crewmen pass their off-duty time with a game of chess. Top right: An officer in his cabin. Bottom left: Cooks prepare a meal in the galley. Bottom right: 'Nightime' conditions.

NO SMOKING

Abandon Ship!

No matter how well submarines are built, and how careful the men who run them, accidents happen. Submarines operate in a far more hostile world than surface ships. If disaster strikes when the craft is deeply submerged, there is little the crew can do except wait hopefully for a search and rescue vessel. In fairly shallow water the submariners can escape without outside help (see below).

After the *Thresher* disaster in 1963, the US Navy quickly set about designing and building a DSRV (Deep Submergence Rescue Vessel), which would be able to rescue the crew of a disabled nuclear submarine in deep water. Giant transport aircraft fly the DSRV to the port nearest the stricken submarine. It is then taken by a surface support ship or by submarine to the scene of the accident. DSRV descends to the disabled craft, using sonar, television and advanced navigation aids to find the craft, and to get precisely into position above the sunken submarine's escape hatch. It has to manoeuvre very gently and accurately. To achieve this, there is a stern propeller which can be angled, for steering, and 'side thrusters' at both sides fore and aft.

Once in position, the DSRV's skirt seals onto the escape hatch. Water is then pumped out of the skirt, and the submariners can open their escape hatch and climb into the DSRV. Twenty four passengers board the submersible, which returns to the mother submarine.

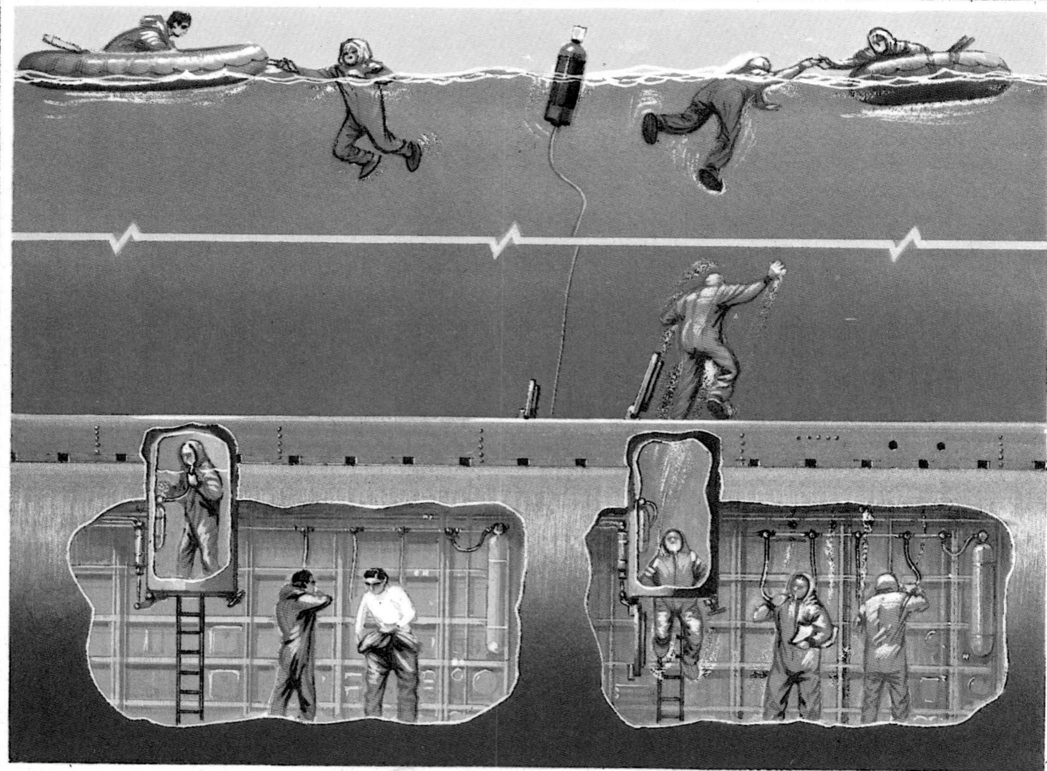

In water up to 100m (300ft) deep, a crew can escape using individual airlocks (left of picture). This takes time, so special air lock compartments have been developed (right). Situated at bow and stern, the men gather in the compartment and seal it with water-tight doors. They then put on their escape suits. Each man plugs a breathing tube into air sockets in the wall. The compartment is flooded with sea water by opening a valve. Once the compartment is completely flooded the escape hatch can be opened. The men disconnect their breathing tubes, and float to the surface.

NUCLEAR SUBMARINE DISASTERS

In April 1963 the American nuclear submarine *Thresher* was undergoing diving trials after a major overhaul. A steep diving manoeuvre somehow got out of control. The crew could do nothing to bring the craft out of the dive. She plunged to the sea bed just 320 km (200 miles) from the American coast, at a point where the water was around two kilometres (1 mile) deep. At the time no craft existed which could go to her assisstance. There are still none today. Even if there were, they would be unable to help. *Thresher* and her crew were beyond assistance immediately after the accident. The enormous pressure of the sea water at that depth crushed her into a tangled heap of twisted steel. Her entire crew of 129 men died in the disaster.

The US Navy immediately began a search for *Thresher*. They knew roughly where she had gone down, but to locate her exactly at such great depth was like looking for a needle in a haystack. The operation took a full four months, and was only possible with the help of the world's deepest-diving research vessel – the bathyscaphe *Trieste* (see page 25).

The DSRV is rescuing the crew from a disabled submarine. It will take seven round trips, about 17 hours, to rescue a full crew. The DSRV is 15 m (50 ft) long and can operate at a depth of 1500 m (5000 ft). The US Navy is working on a massive craft capable of recovering an entire submarine from the seabed.

Working Underwater

Inside submarines and submersibles the crew live in an atmosphere much the same as we do. The exact mixture of the air and its pressure can be fully controlled. Whenever possible, men working underwater work in similar completely sealed containers. The picture shows how this is done on a seabed oil pipeline. The men submerge to the site in a submersible which locks onto a sealed chamber on the pipeline. They transfer from one to the other and work just as they would on the surface. Sometimes a submersible equipped with robot arms can be used where there is no permanent seabed chamber.

Sometimes a job can only be done by a diver. In deep water he works in a metal atmospheric diving suit. The diver is sealed in at normal pressure. But the suit is heavy and bulky and the diver has to operate robot hands. In shallower water divers work in frogmen suits. In these, the diver is not protected from the water pressure. He must work and breathe at that pressure. This means that he must breathe special gas. He cannot return to normal pressure without a spell in a decompression chamber.

The French DS-2 *is looking for a suitable spot to lay a pipeline from the oilrig. The* DS-2 *is driven by two men lying on their stomachs and it is propelled by water jets. The US* Beaver IV *is approaching a pipeline, to complete some delicate work by means of its manipulator arms.*

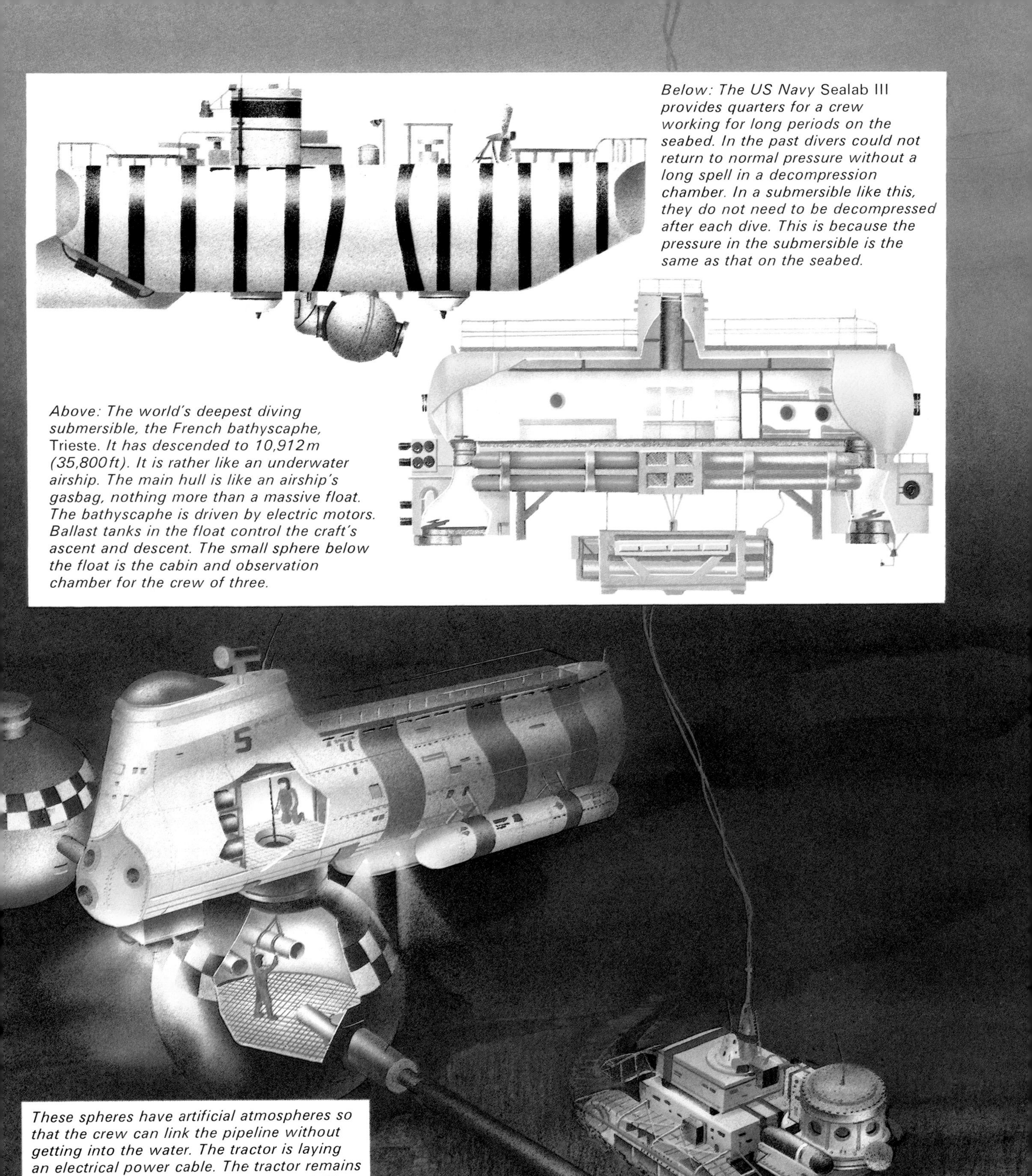

Below: The US Navy Sealab III *provides quarters for a crew working for long periods on the seabed. In the past divers could not return to normal pressure without a long spell in a decompression chamber. In a submersible like this, they do not need to be decompressed after each dive. This is because the pressure in the submersible is the same as that on the seabed.*

Above: The world's deepest diving submersible, the French bathyscaphe, Trieste. *It has descended to 10,912m (35,800ft). It is rather like an underwater airship. The main hull is like an airship's gasbag, nothing more than a massive float. The bathyscaphe is driven by electric motors. Ballast tanks in the float control the craft's ascent and descent. The small sphere below the float is the cabin and observation chamber for the crew of three.*

These spheres have artificial atmospheres so that the crew can link the pipeline without getting into the water. The tractor is laying an electrical power cable. The tractor remains on the seabed until its work is finished. The crew rise and descend in the module which locks on at the back. The tractor is controlled from the module.

For the Future

The picture shows what the naval submarine of the future may look like. It is larger than today's craft–large enough to carry its own mini-submersible in a hold near the bow. This would be valuable for scouting duties, and in rescue and repair operations. The submarine's great size would also give the crew more living space, and it would enable larger and more powerful missiles to be carried.

The artist has shown a craft which is propelled by a jet of water. Water is sucked in and is pushed out again by turbines powered by steam produced by heat from a nuclear-fusion reactor. Today's nuclear submarines have nuclear fission reactors which produce dangerous nuclear waste. A fusion reactor will produce no waste at all.

Huge nuclear-powered submarines of the future may find peaceful duties as cargo carriers. They would have two advantages over surface vessels. First, there are no storms deep underwater. Second, on some journeys nuclear submarines can follow much shorter routes by travelling under the polar ice.

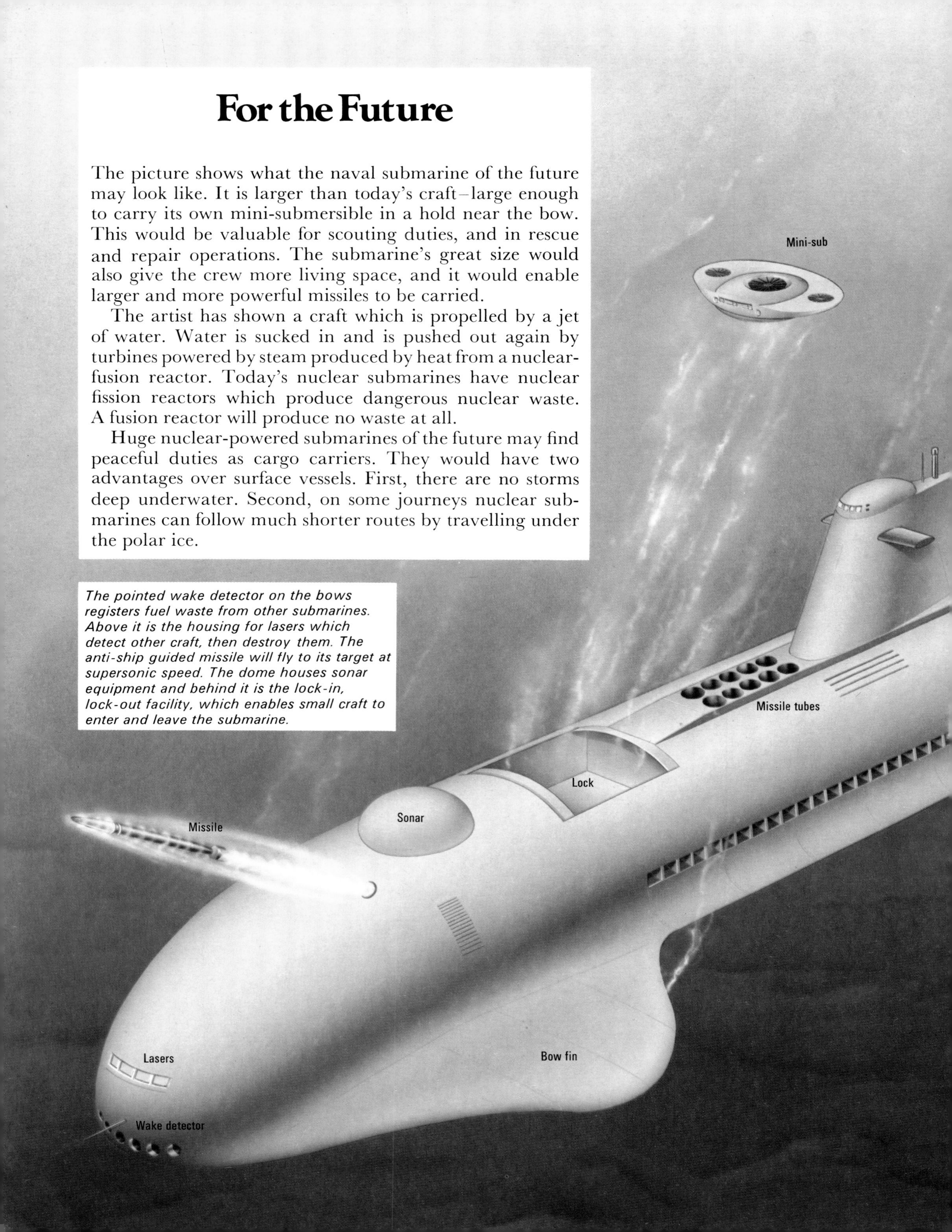

The pointed wake detector on the bows registers fuel waste from other submarines. Above it is the housing for lasers which detect other craft, then destroy them. The anti-ship guided missile will fly to its target at supersonic speed. The dome houses sonar equipment and behind it is the lock-in, lock-out facility, which enables small craft to enter and leave the submarine.

Main picture: From the tubes forward of the fin, the submarine can fire cruise or ballistic missiles. Anti-torpedo decoys are fired from the outlets on the aft edge of the fin. The 'flying saucer'-shaped mini-submarine acts as the captain's barge. On the surface it is a hovercraft. The aft stabilizers are hinged and act as rudders. The steering system is computerized and automatic.

Above: The sabotage squadron is returning to the lock-in facility.

Left: The bow fin has been designed to store a massive array of passive sonar equipment. It also sweeps water towards the intakes along the body of the boat, for the water jet propulsion system.

Fiction Becomes Fact

As long ago as 1870, the French writer Jules Verne (1828–1905) predicted the development of the submarine into the mighty craft we know today.

In his famous book *Twenty Thousand Leagues Under the Sea*, Verne wrote of the adventures of Captain Nemo and the submarine *Nautilus*. It was in Verne's honour that the name *Nautilus* was given to the world's first nuclear-powered submarine, in 1955.

In the future, it seems that fiction is likely to turn into fact. Future submarines will probably be even larger than the latest Ohio and Typhoon craft – which themselves dwarf earlier submarines. Using advanced building methods, the submarines of the future will also be able to dive deeper into the oceans. Computerized navigation systems will guide them unerringly through the darkness of the undersea world.

The submarine in the picture is a military craft. However, such a submarine could also have many peaceful uses. For example, it could carry out scientific research, studying marine life and seeking for minerals on the ocean floor. It could also act as a supply shuttle for permanent manned seabed bases. Huge cargo-carrying submarines towing barges could open up new routes – under the ice caps, for example. And tourists of tomorrow may be able to enjoy a thrilling undersea holiday, exploring the ocean depths in a luxurious submarine-cruiser.

Under the Pole

Left: The USS Whale*, a Sturgeon-class hunter/killer submarine, broke through the ice at the North Pole in 1969. The hydroplanes on the conning tower are in the verical position.*

Below: In May 1986, three US Navy submarines surfaced simultaneously at the North Pole – an unique achievement. Seen here amid the Arctic ice are USS Ray*, USS* Hawkbill *and USS* Archerfish.

In the 1930s, two explorers tried to cross the North Pole in a submarine. They named their vessel *Nautilus*, and fitted it with overhead 'skis'. The idea was that the skis would allow the craft to skid along just below the ice. Their mission failed.

Nearly thirty years later, in 1958, another *Nautilus* set out on the same mission. However, this was the USS *Nautilus* – the world's first nuclear-powered submarine.

In a nuclear submarine, problems of fuel shortage never occur. *Nautilus* had already steamed some 96,000 km (60,000 miles) on a piece of fuel the size of a golf ball. Also, navigation was fairly straightforward as the craft was fitted with the new inertial navigation system which is extremely accurate (see page 10).

Nautilus' voyage was more of a test of endurance and reliability. The mission was top secret, and was nicknamed Operation Sunshine. The submarine set out from Honolulu, and passed under the North Pole just before midnight on 3 August 1958. However, the crew did not radio a message back to base until five days later.

In the meantime, another atomic submarine, the USS *Skate*, had successfully completed another Arctic mission. Its task was to break the ice and surface in polar regions. Two years later, the USS *Triton* completed an even more fantastic mission. It voyaged around the world underwater, following roughly the same route as the famous 16th-century explorer Magellan. Magellan's expedition took three years to sail around the world but *Triton* completed the entire voyage in only 85 days!

Submarines Today

Left: A Soviet Typhoon-class submarine. This is the world's largest submarine, at 20,000 tonnes displacement (as big as a World War II heavy cruiser). Each Typhoon-class submarine carries 20 SS-N-20 missiles with a range of more than 8000 kilometres.

Right: Submarines need well-equipped shore bases to which they can return after patrol for supplies, a fresh crew and routine maintenance. These US submarines are berthed at the Navy submarine base at Point Loma in San Diego Bay.

Left: HMS Churchill *at speed. Like all fleet submarines, it must be capable of high speed to keep up with the surface ships it is designed to protect or hunt. Its whale-like hull gives the submarine good performance both on the surface and submerged.*

Below left: The US Navy's newest and largest nuclear submarines are the Ohio-class. At 18,700 tonnes, the Ohios are smaller than the Soviet Typhoons. Each submarine is armed with 24 Trident missiles (range 7400 kilometres) and carries a crew of 157.

Below: The US Los Angeles-class submarines are high-speed craft designed for anti-submarine warfare. This is the USS Corpus Christi *being launched in 1981.*

IMPORTANT DATES

1620 Cornelius van Drebbel, a Dutchman, builds the first working submarine. It successfully crosses the River Thames in London.
1776 The first attack is made by a submarine, during the American Revolution. The American craft, *Turtle,* fails to destroy its target but returns safely to base.
1800 The American inventor Robert Fulton submerges his experimental submarine *Nautilus* for six hours. The craft arouses little interest, and never sees combat.
1850 An early iron submarine drives Danish fleet away from the shore. Built by Wilhelm Bauer of Germany and called *Brandtaucher,* it has a crew of three and is powered by treadmills. The following year in deep-diving trials, pressure buckles the iron plates and the craft sinks. Bauer and his crew allow the craft to flood, and escape – the first submarine escape.
1863 The first power-driven submarine. This is the French *Plongeur.* Fitted with hydroplanes, and driven by compressed air, it dives to 6 metres (20 feet) but proves to be unstable.
1864 The American *Hunley* becomes the first submarine to sink an enemy ship – but is itself destroyed in the explosion.
1866 Robert Whitehead invents the first practical motorized torpedo – an essential weapon if the submarine was to attack an enemy ship without itself being blown up.
1879 An English clergyman, G.W. Garret builds a steam-powered submarine *Resurgam.*
1886 The first really practical submarine, the French *Gymnote.* It has a cigar-shaped steel hull and electric propulsion, and is the first submarine with effective hydroplanes.
1897 The USS *Holland,* the forerunner of modern non-nuclear submarines, is launched. It has petrol engines and electric motors, and is used by both the US and Royal navies.
1898 US engineer Simon Lake builds a bottom-crawling wheeled submarine called *Argonaut.* From it, he takes the first underwater photographs.
1899 The French *Narval* is completed. It has a double hull, and a high surface speed of 11 knots.
1900 The US Navy takes delivery of its first *Holland* submarine, followed in 1901 by Britain.
1906 The German Navy orders its first *unterseeboot,* the *U-1,* powered by kerosene/electric motors.
1914 Only weeks after the outbreak of World War I, the German U-boat *U-9* sinks three British cruisers off the Dutch coast.
1915 The German submarine *U-20* sinks the liner *Lusitania* in the Atlantic.
1916 The German submarine *Deutschland* crosses the Atlantic.
1917 German U-boats prove that submarines can seriously threaten shipping in wartime.
1930s First midget submarines developed, in Italy and Japan. The most effective in World War II were the British X-craft.
1933 The Dutch officer Jan Wichers invents the breathing tube, or snorkel.
1939–1945 World War II. Submarines play a major part. Britain had 218 and lost 76. Germany had 1072 and lost 705. Japan had 181 and lost 130. The USA had 288 and lost 52. The USSR had 218 and lost 110.
1944 Japanese *1-400*-class submarines, at 3600 tonnes (3500 tons) are the largest submarines built in the pre-nuclear age. Each carries an aircraft, but these are of little use.
1944 Two important new weapons for use against submarines are introduced: the Magnetic Anomaly Detector (MAD) to detect a submerged metal object, and the sonobuoy (a radio-controlled sonar device dropped from an aircraft).
1952 USS *Albacore* is the first submarine to be designed with a 'teardrop' hull shape, for high speed under water.
1955 Soviet *Zulu*-class submarines are the first to carry ballistic missiles to sea, though missiles are short-range.
1955 The world's first nuclear-powered vessel, the USS *Nautilus,* is launched.
1958 *Nautilus* cruises under the North Pole.
1959 The USS *Triton,* the first submarine with two nuclear reactors, is launched. In the following year it circumnavigates the world under water.
1960 USS *George Washington* successfully test-fires the first Polaris missile.
1961 USS *Skyjack* class nuclear submarines are the fastest yet, breaking the 30-knot barrier under water.
1963 Britain's first nuclear submarine, *Dreadnought,* is completed.
1967 Britain's first Polaris submarine, HMS *Resolution,* is commissioned.
1971 France's first nuclear missile-firing submarine, *Redoubtable,* enters service.
1978 US missile-firing submarines are adapted to carry the longer-range Poseidon missile. This increases the number of possible targets for each submarine from 16 (with Polaris) to 160 (each Poseidon missile has 10 warheads).
1980 Launch of the latest US submarine class, the *Ohio,* armed with 24 Trident missiles. At 18,300 tonnes (18,000 tons) *Ohio* is dwarfed by Soviet *Typhoon* giant submarines, also launched in 1980, which displace 20,000 tonnes (19,700 tons).

GLOSSARY OF TERMS

Aft At or near the stern of a ship.

Air Lock Double door through which people or objects can enter or leave a submerged vessel without flooding it.

Amidships The centre section of a vessel.

Aqualung Self-contained underwater breathing apparatus, or scuba gear, as worn by frogmen.

Attitude The position of a submarine under water, affected by movements such as roll, pitch and yaw.

ASW Anti-Submarine Warfare.

Ballast tank Water tank which can be filled or emptied for diving and surfacing.

Ballistic missile Rocket-powered weapon that flies out beyond the Earth's atmosphere and follows a curving path before descending on its target.

Beam The width of a ship at its widest point.

Bends The formation of bubbles of gas in a diver's blood if he changes too quickly from high pressure under water to normal air pressure.

Bow The front of a ship.

Bridge Area on top of the fin of a submarine from which the vessel is commanded when surfaced.

Bulkhead Wall dividing the inside of a ship's hull.

Buoyancy The ability of an object to float.

Chart A map of the seabed and coastal waters.

Communications Buoy Floating buoy that receives recorded messages or other radio signals from a submerged submarine, and relays these to an aircraft.

Conning tower The fin (or superstructure) of a submarine, that rises above the water.

Cruise missile Missile that flies at a very low height to make radar detection difficult.

Decompression chamber Sealed chamber in which a diver remains while adjusting to high underwater pressure to normal air pressure.

Depth charge Underwater bomb dropped into the sea to attack a submarine.

Diesel-electric engine Propulsion system used in pre-nuclear and modern conventional submarines.

DSRV Deep Submergence Rescue Vessel.

Dunking Technique by which a helicopter lowers a listening device into the sea to detect a submarine.

Electrolysis Process by which oxygen can be made by passing an electric current through water.

Escape hatch Means of escape for submarine crews trapped below the surface.

Fathom Nautical measure, equal to 1.8 metres (6 feet).

Fin The streamlined conning tower, or sail, of a modern submarine.

Galley Ship's kitchen.

Harpoon Type of sea-skimming anti-ship missile fired from a submarine.

Hatch Opening or door in a ship's hull.

Heads Naval term for lavatories.

Hull The body of a ship.

Hydrophone A listening device that detects the sound of a submarine's engines under water.

Hydroplane Small wing-like fin used for controlling a submarine's angle and depth.

Knot Measure of speed used at sea, equal to one nautical mile per hour. One knot equals about 1.8 kilometres an hour (1.15 miles per hour).

MAD Magnetic Anomaly Detector. This picks up the presence of metal objects, such as a submarine, under water.

Mess Where naval crewmen have their meals.

Nautical mile Measure of distance used at sea. It equals 1852 metres (2025 yards).

Periscope System of mirrors that allows a submarine captain to look above the surface of the water while his craft remains hidden.

Port The left-hand side of a ship, looking forward.

Radar System that detects distant objects by bouncing radio beams off them and recording the echoes it receives.

Radio letters Messages sent by crewmen's families by radio to submarine crews on long patrols.

Rudder Upright metal blade at the stern, which can be angled for turning the vessel.

Sail Another name for the conning tower, or fin.

Screw Submarine's propellor.

Scuba Diver's breathing gear. The initials stand for Self Contained Underwater Breathing Apparatus.

Seabed sensor Electronic device placed on the seabed to listen and watch for passing submarines.

Sextant Optical instrument used in celestial navigation for finding the angle of a star from the horizon or from the vertical.

Side thruster Small propellor used to thrust water out at either side for steering.

Silent running Procedure used to reduce noise inside a submerged submarine, in order to avoid detection.

SINS Ship's Inertial Navigational System.

Snorkel, or **Snort-mask** Breathing tube through which submarines can take in fresh air and get rid of stale air and fumes without surfacing.

Sonar Echo-sounding system used to detect objects under water.

Starboard The right-hand side of a ship looking forward.

Stern The back of a ship.

Submersible Submarine craft used for scientific and industrial tasks.

SUBROC Type of anti-submarine missile fired from a hunter/killer submarine.

Superstructure Parts of a ship built on or above the main hull.

Thermocline Ocean layer where warm and cold waters mix, distorting underwater sound waves and providing a good hiding place for a submarine.

Torpedo Underwater self-propelled weapon.

Trailing aerial Radio aerial at the end of a long wire trailed behind the submarine to receive radio signals.

Trident A type of submarine-launched ballistic missile (SLBM).

Trim The way a ship floats in the water (e.g. on an even keel, down at the bow, etc.).

Trim tank Water tank which can be more or less filled with water to trim a vessel.

VLF Very Low Frequency radio waves. These can penetrate water, though not to great depths, or over long distances.

Ward room Officers' living room on board a warship.

Watch The name for a crewman's spell of duty.

OTHER BOOKS TO READ

Submarines by Richard Garrett. Weidenfeld & Nicholson
Submarines by Richard Compton-Hall. Wayland.
Submarines in Colour by Bill Gunston. Blandford.
Submarines by Heinz Kurth. World's Work
The British Submarine by F.W. Lipscomb. A & C. Black
Exploring Under the Sea by Brian Williams. Piccolo
A Pictorial History of Oceanographic Submersibles by James B. Sweeney. Robert Hale
Nuclear Submarine by Mike Rossiter. Collins

INDEX

PHOTOGRAPHIC ACKNOWLEDGEMENTS

The publishers wish to thank the following for supplying photographs for this book: Page 2 Ministry of Defence (MOD); *top* Mary Evans; *bottom* Mansell Collection; 8 Daily Telegraph; 10 MOD; 12 Daily Telegraph; 13 Lockheed Missiles & Space Co Inc; 14 ZEFA; 16 Daily Telegraph; 17 *top and bottom left* MOD/Royal Navy/Military Archive & Research Services Inc (MARS); *top right* Fleet PRO, Royal Navy; *bottom right* COI; 24 US Navy/MARS; 25 US Navy, Washington DC; 26 *top* US Navy, Washington DC; *bottom* ZEFA; 27 *top* ZEFA; *bottom left* US Navy, Washington DC; *bottom right* US Navy/MARS; 30 Wood Hole Oceanographic Institute.